POGO'S
BODY POLITIC
by Walt Kelly

EDITED BY SELBY KELLY

A Fireside Book Published by

Simon and Schuster

For Herblock
and all the others
who with inkpot and typewriter
help us keep our eyes
on the public pose,
posturing and positions
of political persons

Contents

Foreword

Walt Kelly, who knew all the pundits and politicos of his day, spent most of his non-working time with the journalists and writers who were his boon companions and friends. Jimmy Breslin, who was one of them, contributes this reminiscence.

Walt Kelly had a unique mind, and we're lucky that so many of his notions continue to live in his books. He accomplished a lot with those political cartoons of his—Pogo is a great invention, a great character.

Walt's humor came from the generalized comedy of human beings trying to be important, and his natural target was politicians. He had this unique view of human politics and how it worked—the buffoonery of people trying to look solemn and important who were actually out doing evil things.

He would look about when he came to Washington in the rain, notice the sea of limousines—and realize that people in government never get wet! Kelly knew what it was to get wet, and he'd look at the pomposity of those people and capture them brilliantly. He had that magnificent formal swamp (Okefenokee), and he could always drag them down there and make them more evil than any character in that swamp ever was—dirtier and uglier.

In an odd way, he had a real attachment for the great villains of our time—Joe McCarthy or Agnew or Mitchell. It was great! Kelly would be doing the strip and then McCarthy would go out and do something crazy, and that would give us another two or three weeks of comic strips. It was marvelous. When McCarthy died, Kelly cried as though he'd lost his best friend. Nixon came along but couldn't quite fill the bill; in a funny way, Agnew came closest.

The strip was so good because he'd catch the true imbecility of people; he'd make you laugh. The best thing I saw him do in my time was a strip for the New York *Tribune* about Wallace and the Ku Klux Klan. He had the Klan guys taking off their hoods one by one, and he made them so ugly that by the last panel Congress was trying to pass a Federal law to make them put the hoods back on.

His was a completely original mind, with those ideas of his coming fast and furious, shooting over the rim of his glass at the bar (we spent a lot of time in bars) or over his shoulder as he stomped out. It was dazzling to see that mind at work. Not that he was so consistently gentle, so predictably pleasant, when he was around. He was like Irish weather. In places in that country there is a light rain which changes into a warm sunbath which dissolves into a fierce Atlantic storm all within the hour . . . Kelly was that piece of Irish sky.

Kelly probably made a lot of money over the years, but he didn't care about money, he just gave it away. He took care of everybody but himself—that he wouldn't do. He always told me that it did not matter how long you lived; the important thing was how far you got. Well, he got far enough; the pity is that he did not live very long. In this he was very thoughtless, because original minds arrive in our midst only every quarter of a century or so, and if they leave us too soon, as Kelly did, we are in trouble.

JIMMY BRESLIN
1976

CHAPTER

1

OH, TO FLEA
OR NOT TO FLEA...

CHAPTER

2

AH, WHAT A GOSSAMER WEB HE'D WEAVE...

YOU'LL RECALL I CAME ABOARD TO WITNESS THE PERSISTENCE OF THE SPIDER WHO TAUGHT ROBERT BRUCE TO PERSEVERE.

AN ANCESTOR OF MINE.

ONCE HE CAST ··· TWICE ··· THRICE ··· FRICE ··· FIVE TIMES ··· SIX TIMES HE CAST ···

AYE! AYE!

THEN, ON THE SEVENTH CAST ··· SUCCESS!

YEA

HE HIT HIS POINT, COLLECTED THE POT AND RETIRED TO A DUKEDOM IN IRELAND.

YOU HAVE THE WRONG FAILURE IN MIND WHEN YOU SPEAK OF A DICE PLAYING SPIDER ···

WELL, I COME FROM A LONG STRING OF SUCCESSFUL FAILURES ···

THIS CHAP WHO ENCOURAGED ROBERT BRUCE, TRIED SIX TIMES AND FAILED, YOU SAY ··· WELL, THAT WAS HARRY MacSPIDER ···

25

26

3

SNOOZY SNOO-YEAR, RISE AN' SHINE

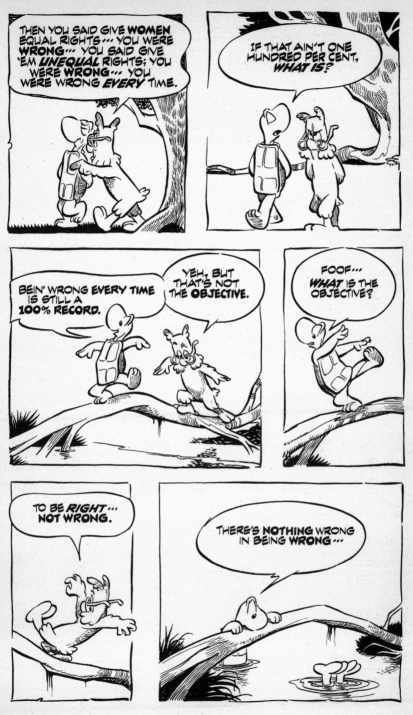

CHAPTER

4

FOR A
SOGGY VALENTINE

CHAPTER

5

WHERE THERE'S A *WONT*, THERE'S A *WILL*

WHERE THERE'S A RHYME, THERE'S A REASON

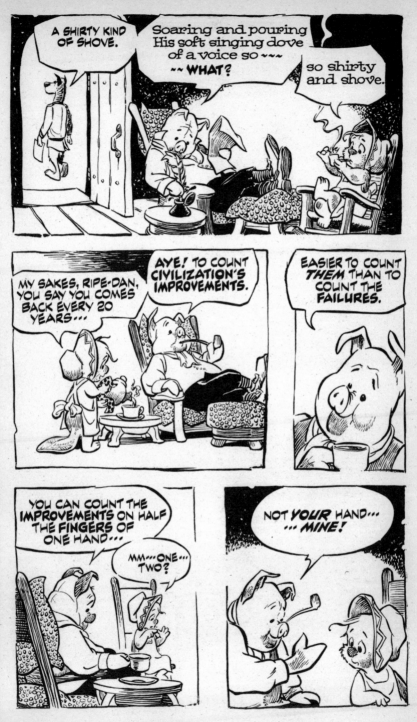

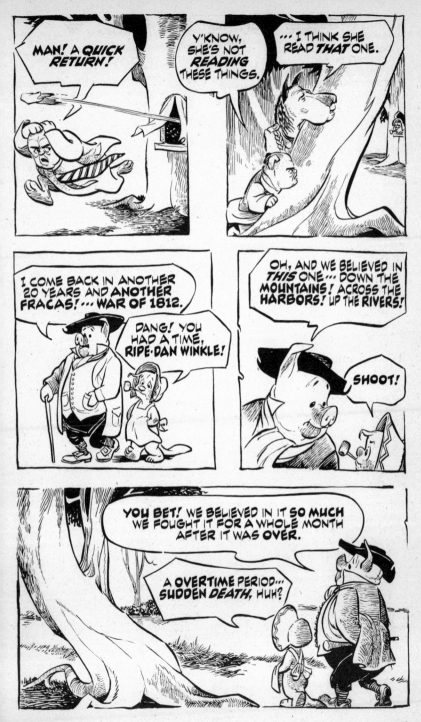

45

ENEMIES IN
THE MESSAGE PARLOR,
COUNTIN' OUT THE LOYAL

47

48

8

SUCCESS IN THE HARD LUCK DEPARTMENT

53

9

THIS CLASSY-FILED AD'S
A SLEEPER

10

CELESTIAL CONTRACT
WITHOUT
CEREBRAL CONTACT

58

59

CHAPTER

11

HARD MUSH
AND ERSATZ LUCK

CHAPTER
12
A HITCH
IN THE POSTAL SERVICE

CHAPTER

13

THROW THE RASCALS
IN, OUT, OR UP

14

ALL THE NEWS
THAT'LL FIT

CHAPTER

15

GETTIN' A BOOT
OUTA FISHIN'

HE EXPLAINS THAT THE **LONGEST WAY 'ROUND** IS THE **SHORTEST WAY HOME**....

....SO THEY SHOOK HANDS ALL AROUND.....

....IN FAREWELL, AND EXPLAINED THAT GOOMIS HADN'T BEEN **EXACTLY** ON HIS WAY **HOME**....

OL' TED DUREIN

PENINSULA HERALD

OL' RIPE-DAN WINKLE WENT BACK TO HIS MOUNTAIN, COMPLAININ' THAT THINGS IS **WORSE'N** THEY WAS COUPLE **GENERATIONS** AGO.

HE'S RIGHT.

CALIF.

THE S.S. SCOTT DALEY

HOW COME?

THE **DOLLAR'S SMALLER**.... THE **BOMB'S BIGGER.**

17

THE F.O.O.F.
FOOF-ARAW

CHAPTER
18
THE BOYS AND THE BEES
AND THE BOOM
THAT BOMBED

94

CHAPTER

19

HIDDEN HUMANS:
A SECRET SURVEY

100

101

102

20

SENATOR BULFROG
FLIPS HIS WIG

107

WELL... WHY NOT?

...HE'S RICHLY ENDOWED WITH THE PROPER EQUIPMENT.

I BE DOGGED! IT'S SENATOR BULFROG!

RIGHT ON SCHEDULE... ELECTION DAY!

Hail, fellow Toilers in our Patriotic Vineyards.

Aye, fellow workers for the Common Weal! I've been busy voting on this glorious day~~

It took all morn to vote my private List from the dead center of Town~~ The Cemetery!

THAT'S ILLEGAL!

Fie, Sirrah! Would you then disenfranchise the noble Dead?! For Shame!

108

CHAPTER
21
A BEDBUG IS A BEDBUG, BUT A MOUSE IS A FROG IS A TOAD

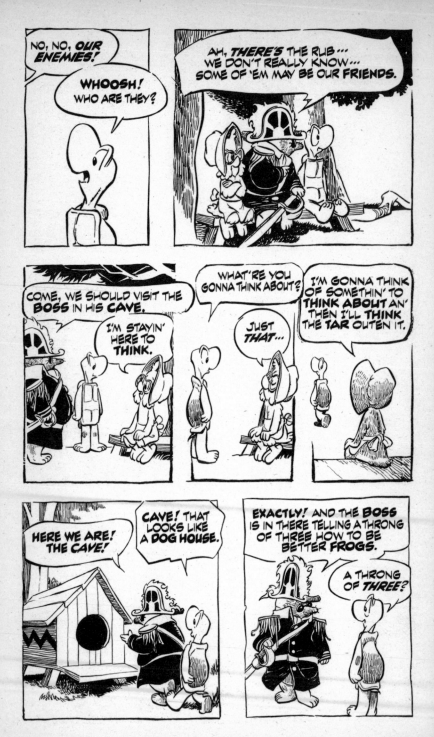

117

119

NO, BUT *HE* IS.

AWRIGHT! OFF TO THE RIFLE RANGE!

AFTER ALL, WHEN HE GIVES AN *ORDER*, HOW'S HE GOING TO KNOW WHAT IT IS IF HE CAN'T *HEAR* IT?

THAT FELLOW BACK THERE TEACHIN' THEM FROGS TO BE *MICE* ···· WHAT'S HE KNOW ABOUT IT?

HE'S A FROG HIMSELF.

THERE YOU GO! A REMARK BY THE USUALLY UNINFORMED MIND ···· A SNAP *JUDGEMENT!* THAT MAN MAY *LOOK* LIKE A FROG ···· BUT ON *MICE* HE'S AN EXPERT.

HE'S A *CAT?*

HE'S A *TOAD.*

SEE!?

120

CHAPTER

22

ANOTHER UNDEREMPLOYED SLEEPER

123

125

126

127

CHAPTER

23

EXIT